POLLS APART

How to Tell a Democrat from a Republican

Kathi Paton
and
Bill Plympton

Dolphin Books
Doubleday & Company, Inc.
Garden City, New York
1984

Special thanks to editor David Gernert and designer James Kiehle.

This Dolphin Books edition is the first publication of POLLS APART.

Library of Congress Cataloging in Publication Data

Paton, Kathi.
  Polls apart.

  (Dolphin books)
    1. United States—Politics and government—1945-   —Caricatures and
cartoons. 2. Democratic Party (U.S.)—Caricatures and cartoons. 3. Republican
Party (U.S.: 1854-   )—Caricatures and cartoons. 4. American wit and humor,
Pictorial. I. Plympton, Bill. II. Title.
E839.5.P325 1984   324.273′0207   83-25367
ISBN 0-385-19488-9

To our parents

Bernice and Bill Paton, Republicans

and

Wilda and Don Plympton, Democrats

Preamble

W hen in the course of human events it became necessary for one political party to distinguish itself from another, cartoonist Thomas Nast obliged. His satiric drawings of the 1870's were the first to show the Democratic party as a wild jackass and the GOP as a jumbo elephant. Eventually the parties accepted Nast's labels, despite a grass-roots attempt during the 1920 presidential campaign of Democrat James Cox to adopt a less risible emblem: a rooster supposedly crowing about "the dawn of a new era." Men and women all over the country sported chickens in their lapels that year. Both Cox and cocks were defeated, losing to Warren Harding and his notoriously neological promise to lead the country "back to normalcy." Since then jumbo and jackass have reigned unchallenged.

N aturally, to assume that the powers that be are always Democrats or Republicans would be to ignore the declaration of independents. Know-Nothing, Prohibition, Anti-Monopoly, and National Silver tickets have all bid for the highest office in the land. Socialist Eugene Debs won nearly a million votes for President the same year Cox was crowing—and Debs was campaigning from a cell in a federal penitentiary. But in this century the climax of the American political pageant has always been a coronation where the hats are labeled "Democrat" or "Republican." Not many people still fret about the difference between a Know-Nothing and a National Silver. All of us pause to wonder what sets off a Democrat from a Republican.

T he causes which impel this separation into parties can be reduced to the need to be different from, and therefore better than, the other guy. The need becomes a compulsion when the candidates are as similar as Tweedledum and Tweedledee. Even journalists—especially journalists—become confused when the race gets close and dirty. Witness the remark of New York *Tribune* editor Horace Greeley, who was once nominated for the presidency by both parties: "I never said all Democrats were saloonkeepers. What I said was that all saloonkeepers were Democrats." Clearly, a field guide to the American voter is long overdue.

W e hold this truth to be self-evident: It's high time we had a few pointers on how to tell an ass from an elephant. Who knows whether Aunt Louise, a rock-ribbed Republican, actually pulls the lever for the Grand Old Party? With *Polls Apart*, you can pull aside the last remaining symbol of privacy in the land—the voting-booth curtain—and find out the *real* differences between Democrats and Republicans. Now everyone will know which party line his neighbor is on ,as well as the true direction of his own political leanings. Of course, directions can shift.

A ll men are created equal, endowed by their Creator with certain inalienable rights, including the right to switch parties. Republican Abraham Lincoln came from a long line of Democrats, and Jacqueline Kennedy Onassis once said, "You have to have been a Republican to know how good it is to be a Democrat." Before you decide to jump the fence, figure out which side you're on.

L ife, liberty, and the pursuit of a few spirited laughs is what this hedonist's dream—membership in a perpetual party—is all about.

Kathi Paton
New York City
1983

The Democrat's ancestors came to America
in the hold of a European ship.

The Republican's ancestors
arrived the same way.

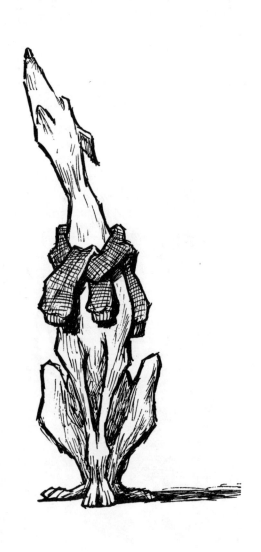

Republican dog.

Democratic dog.

Democrats have a rich family history.

Republicans also have a rich family history.

Republicans kissing.

Democrats kissing.

Democrats go to Europe and
look up distant relatives.

Republicans go to Europe and look
up American restaurants.

Republicans believe in plastic.

Democrats believe in plastic.

Democratic sleeping attire.

Republican sleeping attire.

A Republican's liquid assets.

A Democrat's liquid assets.

The Democratic family's front yard.

The Republican family's front yard.

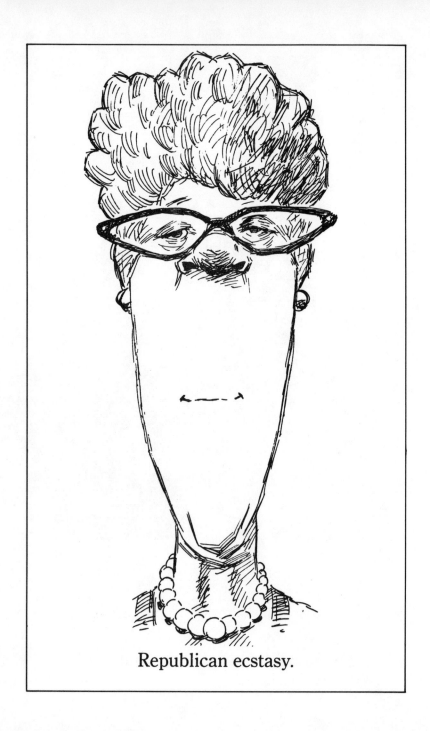

Republican ecstasy.

Democratic ecstasy.

Democrats tape up drawings
by their children.

Republicans purchase art recommended
by their investment bankers.

Republicans chase foxes in the
small hours of the morning.

Democrats chase foxes in even
smaller hours of the morning.

Democrats never forget to
leave a tip.

Republicans never forget to
leave a tip either.

Political scandal, Republican style.

Political scandal, Democratic style.

When Democrats face a personal crisis,
they switch psychiatrists.

When Republicans face a personal
crisis, they switch brokers.

Woman staying in shape
the Republican way.

Woman staying in shape
the Democratic way.

Democrats love inspired music.

Republicans love inspired music.

Republicans vacation in the
Caribbean in winter.

Democrats vacation in the
Caribbean in summer.

A sex symbol for Democrats.

A sex symbol for Republicans.

Republicans dream of a spot on the 500.

Democrats dream of a spot at the 500.

Democratic fathers take
their sons on camping trips to tell them
about the birds and the bees.

Republican fathers take
their sons to the stock exchange to tell
them about puts and calls.

Republicans enjoy a drink now and then.

Democrats also enjoy a drink now and then.

Democratic bumper stickers.

Republican bumper stickers.

Republicans believe in an effective
national defense.

Democrats also believe in an
effective national defense.

Sex, Democratic style.

Sex, Republican style.

Republican members of the jet set.

Democratic members of the Jet set.

Democrats can't bear rejection.

Republicans can't bear rejection either.

Republicans appreciate the beauty
of bodies in motion.

Democrats also appreciate the beauty
of bodies in motion.

The Democrat's favorite actor is
George C. Scott— in *Dr. Strangelove*.

The Republican's favorite actor is
George C. Scott —in *Patton*.

A Republican's club insignia.

A Democrat's club insignia.

Democrat on a fishing trip.

Republican on a fishing trip.

A teenage date, Republican style.

A teenage date, Democratic style.

Democrats think the last great
President was Roosevelt.

Republicans think the last great
President was Roosevelt.

Republican kids enjoy water sports.

Democratic kids enjoy water sports.

Democratic mixed marriage.

Republican mixed marriage.

Republican "youngster."

Democratic "youngster."

Democrats try to save animals.

Republicans wear animals.

Republican campaign handshake.

Democratic campaign handshake.

Democrats read paperbacks.

Republicans buy hardcovers.

Republicans enjoying the ponies.

Democrats enjoying the ponies.

Effective discipline by Democratic mothers.

Effective discipline by Republican mothers.

Republican children have
ballet lessons, tennis lessons, music lessons,
and riding lessons.

Democratic children have
brothers and sisters.

A big family dinner, Democratic style.

A big family dinner, Republican style.

Republicans hate foreign dictators
who are left-wing fanatics.

Democrats hate foreign dictators
who are right-wing fanatics.

Democrat voting.

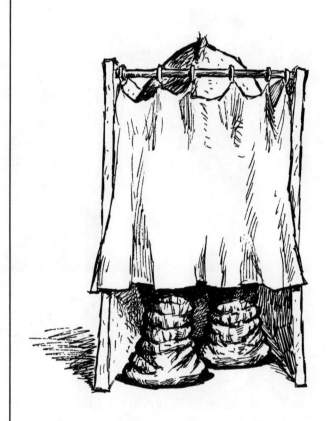

Republican voting.

ALEX GOTFRYD

Kathi Paton is currently a book editor at a New York publishing house. A former newspaper reporter, she is the author of a play, a movie script, magazine articles, and handmade books in very limited editions.

Bill Plympton's cartoon strip is syndicated by Universal Press. His drawings have appeared in national magazines and humor anthologies, and have been collected in two books. Bill's current project is *Boomtown*, an animated antinuclear film written by Jules Feiffer. He was born in Oregon and now lives in New York.